CONTENTS

INTRODUCTION

I don't know why my parents named me Hunter. Maybe they knew I'd become a detective and hunt down clues. Or maybe I wanted to be a detective because of my name. Not that I'm an official detective. I'm just a twelve-year-old who loves to solve mysteries. The twistier, the better.

My brother, Logan, likes to solve them, too. He's two years older and a lot more popular. I'm the shy one. I like to stay in the background, at least at this point in my life. Even when I solve a mystery on my own, I usually let Logan take credit.

You're probably wondering what kind of cases we get here in Clifton Lake. We don't have any murders that I know of. We do have our share of robberies and vandalism and a few mysteries that aren't really crimes, just puzzling things that happen.

Some of our cases come from helping friends who know about our special skills. Others come from Mom, who is the principal of our middle school. Whenever strange things happen there, she turns to us. Plus, there's our uncle, Officer J.B. Monroe of the Clifton Lake Police Department. He's known for his talent at solving cases, even though Logan and I have solved a few of them for him.

Maybe someday I'll become confident enough to take credit for my deductions. But for now I'm happy.

So, these are the cases that Logan and I solved. I end each story right before the solution, just in case you want to play along and solve them yourself. Whether you think you know the answer or you're stumped, turn to the back of the book to find out who did it and why. Happy sleuthing!

The Case of the

ghostly note

& Other Solve-It-Yourself

whodunits

Hy Conrad

MoonDance

Inspiring | Educating | Creating | Entertaining

Brimming with creative inspiration, how-to projects, and useful information to enrich your everyday life, Quarto Knows is a favorite destination for those pursuing their interests and passions. Visit our site and dig deeper with our books into your area of interest: Quarto Creates, Quarto Cooks, Quarto Homes, Quarto Lives, Quarto Drives, Quarto Explores, Quarto Gifts, or Quarto Kids.

© 2017 Quarto Publishing Group USA Inc.
Text © 2017 Hy Conrad

First Published in 2017 by MoonDance Press, an imprint of The Quarto Group.
6 Orchard Road, Suite 100, Lake Forest, CA 92630, USA.
T (949) 380-7510 **F** (949) 380-7575 **www.QuartoKnows.com**

MoonDance Press titles are also available at discount for retail, wholesale, promotional, and bulk purchase. For details, contact the Special Sales Manager by email at specialsales@quarto.com or by mail at The Quarto Group, Attn: Special Sales Manager, 401 Second Avenue North, Suite 310, Minneapolis, MN 55401 USA.

ISBN: 978-1-63322-350-9

Cover design and layout by Melissa Gerber
Illustrations by Jomike Tejido

Printed in China
10 9 8 7 6 5 4 3 2 1

WHO EMPTIED THE CANDY JAR?

Ginny hands out the big homemade cookies, each one sealed in a plastic baggie. "It's Mom's recipe. We can sell them door-to-door."

Ginny has brought along samples, one for each kid on the committee. Then she looks at me and frowns. "Sorry, Hunter. I should have brought an extra one for you."

"That's okay," I say.

I really don't mind. I like being ignored while my big brother, Logan, and his friends do their thing. Their "thing" right now is raising money for band uniforms at our middle school. Logan shares his cookie with me as they talk about ways to make money.

"Great cookie," says Derrick, who looks like he wants a second one. Derrick always looks like he wants more food.

"Great," echoes Jocelyn. She's the tallest girl in school and the only girl who plays the tuba. "I wish Brian was here. I'm dying to know how we did at Saturday's car wash."

Brian Brown is the band treasurer. His mom called Logan a few minutes ago and said there was some family emergency and that Brian couldn't make it. So it's just the four of them sitting in our living room…plus me.

After the meeting, we all walk over to Brian's to see if everything is all right. But no one is home. There's even a handwritten sign telling us this. You see, Brian's dad is an accountant, and he runs his company from his house. Normally, during business hours, the front door is unlocked for customers to come and go. But now we see that Mr. Brown has taped up a sign saying, "Closed All Day. Family Emergency."

"They must have left in a hurry," I say. Logan is about to ask how I know this, but the answer is simple. I point to the open garage door. "They drove off and forgot to close the garage."

We're still standing on the porch, wondering what to do, when the Browns come home. Their car pulls into the garage and Brian is the first one out. "Grandma Brown broke her hip," he tells us. "We all had to go take care of her in the hospital."

"She'll be okay," adds Mr. Brown. "She's a tough one."

"Why didn't you call and tell us?" Derrick asks. "We were worried."

"We thought you'd be at the meeting," says Ginny.

"I forgot," says Brian. "Mom finally remembered to call, but that was hours later. Sorry."

Mr. and Mrs. Brown disappear into the house, leaving Brian and the rest of us in the garage. It's Jocelyn who first thinks of the possible danger. "You guys left the garage door open? You could have been robbed."

This doesn't seem to be the case. The garage is crowded with all sorts of things. There are shelves all along the back wall covered with boxes and piles of magazines. Brian scans the place. "Looks like we got lucky. Nothing's been taken."

"What about the candy jar?" asks Derrick.

At first I think he just wants candy. But the others know what he's talking about. They all focus on the middle shelf and watch as Brian pulls out a tin candy jar, half hidden between two boxes. He removes the lid and stares inside. "It's gone," Brian gasps. "The money's gone."

Everyone's in shock. Then Logan explains to me that the jar is where Brian keeps the band money before he puts it in the bank. There was almost $200 in there from Saturday's car wash. And now it's gone.

The others start yelling at Brian for keeping the money in such a stupid place, but they all knew where he kept it. So if they really thought it was stupid, they should have said something. Brian feels terribly, but there's nothing we can do. He goes into the house to tell his parents, and the rest of us go home.

"The police are never going to catch the thief," Logan says as the two of us walk back to our house. "A hundred people could have seen the note and the open garage door."

"You're wrong," I say. Logan doesn't mind when I tell him he's wrong. He's used to it. "Nothing was touched in the garage except for the candy jar. The money was taken by someone who knew exactly where Brian kept it."

"You mean someone from the committee?" Logan asks. He can't believe it. "You mean one of my friends stole it? From our own band?"

"They were tempted by the money," I say. "One of them came by Brian's house this morning. They saw the note and the open garage door. They walked right in."

I let this news sink in. We're just coming up to our front door when Logan asks, "Do you know who it was?" This is a normal question. I almost always know who it was.

Do you know the answer?
Who took the money from the candy jar?
What mistake did the thief make?

Solution on page 79

THE KEY TO THE TEST

It's the first really cold day of the school year, and I guess the furnace isn't quite cranked up. We're all shivering in the hallway, but that doesn't stop Logan and his friends from stopping to chat about the big news.

"Someone stole a copy of the standardized test," Pete Lopez whispers.

"I hear the thief is selling the answers," Jocelyn whispers back. "I wonder how much they're charging."

By this point, we've all heard the story. "Come on," says Logan. "You guys would never buy test answers."

"You wouldn't." Pete laughs. "Your mom's the principal."

That's true. Our mother, Mrs. Monroe, is principal of Clifton Lake Middle School. And this is the one year, with me in sixth grade and Logan in eighth, that both her sons are serving time in her school.

I'm standing right by them, wondering if I should go to Mom's office and tell her. I don't want to be a snitch, but this is important. And then I see Mom and Mr. Johnson, the big security guard, heading straight for us. I can tell from her attitude that they already know. All the kids stop talking.

"Logan, what do you know about this?"

"Nothing." Logan hates being caught between Mom and his friends. "I don't even know if it's true."

"It's true," Mom tells us. "I left my desk drawer unlocked this morning when I went for coffee. When I came back, the key to the file cabinet was missing. In the file cabinet, I immediately checked the folder with the statewide tests. All the tests were there—except the last page of the eighth-grade test. I found that page inside the photocopy machine."

Mr. Johnson shakes his head. "Not returning the key?

Leaving a page in the copier? The thief was obviously in a hurry. Sloppy work."

"Who else was in your office this morning?" I ask as I step out of the shadows.

"Good question," Mom says, finally noticing me. Then she turns to Pete and Jocelyn, using that scolding tone principals love. "Perhaps you two can answer him."

It turns out both Pete and Jocelyn were in Mom's office. Pete came by to drop off his permission slip for a school trip. A few minutes later, Jocelyn came in to hand in the marching band's newsletter for approval. It would be hard for either of them to deny being there, since the newsletter and the permission slip were both on Mom's desk when she got back from the teachers' lounge.

"I went in your office for a few seconds," says Pete. "And I didn't touch anything. You can check for fingerprints."

"Me, too," says Jocelyn. "I hung around because I wanted to talk to you about the band uniforms. I sat down and looked at a magazine, but then I had to get to class. I don't think I touched anything else."

"Couldn't someone else have been in your office?" Logan asks.

"It's possible," Mom admits. "But I was only gone for ten minutes."

"Would it help if you searched their lockers?" Logan asks. Both Jocelyn and Pete agree that they have nothing to hide.

Jocelyn is first. She twirls her combination, opens her locker, and stands back. Mom inspects the contents—a few books and notebooks, her coat, a scarf, and a little mirror attached to the back of the locker door. There's nothing incriminating, and everyone breathes a sigh of relief.

Pete's locker is a few feet away. He twirls his own combination and Mr. Johnson inspects the inside of the locker. The security guard pulls out the books stacked on the bottom. All of a sudden, something falls out and clangs onto the floor, right by my feet. It's a little key, and without thinking, I pick it up.

Mom takes it from my hand. "My file cabinet key. Peter?"

"I didn't do it," Pete shouts. "Someone must have planted it."

"Planted it in your locker?" Mom's eyes are full of disappointment. "Who?"

"Jocelyn knows my combination. A lot of kids know each other's combinations."

Everyone starts arguing back and forth, except Logan and me. I catch my brother's eye and pull him aside. "The key was warm when I picked it up."

"So?" he says. "Is that a clue?"

"It's a very big clue."

Are you as smart as Hunter?
Who stole the test answers?
Why is the warm key a clue?

Solution on page 79

HOW TIMMY GOT BETTER

I've been worried about Timmy all day. He's my best friend, and he's been sick a lot this year. First it was the flu, then some stomach problems. He was out of school yesterday and today, so I decide to drop by and see him on my way home.

When I knock on the Olsens' door, I hear his mom on the other side. "Come in!" She's on the phone in the little office in the front of the house—some work stuff, I guess. Goldie, their golden retriever, runs up to greet me, almost knocking me over with her big, dirty paws.

"Hunter." Mrs. Olsen ends her call and apologizes. "Sorry. It's hard doing business from home. I've been on the phone and computer all day."

"No problem." I brush the dirt off my jacket. Mrs. Olsen is a lawyer, but she manages to stay home whenever her son gets sick. "How's Timmy?"

She walks me back to the family kitchen. "He vomited this morning and has a fever. I've been letting him sleep. He'll be so glad to see you." She goes to the back stairs and shouts up. "Timmy! Hunter's here. Do you want any soup?"

"No, thanks," says this soft, raspy voice from upstairs.

Timmy's mother checks the cabinets. "I thought I had some vegetable beef soup, but I guess not. Why don't you take him a brownie?"

"Sure," I say. If Timmy doesn't want a brownie, there'll be more for me.

Mrs. Olsen fixes a tray with brownies and two glasses of milk. Goldie scratches at the back door. But when she sees me going up the back stairs with the tray, she follows, almost knocking me over again.

Timmy is in bed, the covers up to his neck. He's pale and weak looking, and every few seconds he shivers. But he's glad

14

to see me. "Hunter. How was school? I don't know if I'll be able to make it tomorrow. I hope so."

"Pretty boring, huh?"

"I've been in bed all day," he says, "with no one but Mom. And she's working."

Timmy and I split a brownie and talk about school. A few minutes later, we hear Mrs. Olsen calling up the stairs. "Timmy! I'm taking Goldie for a walk. Poor thing hasn't been out since this morning. Goldie!" Goldie hears her name and races out of the room, barking as she goes.

I wait until I hear the door close, glad that there's no one else in the house. "I know you're faking it."

"Faking what?" he says. "I have a fever and the chills. And vomiting. Ask Mom."

"Parents are easy to fool," I say. "You can rub a thermometer between your fingers to get the temperature up. Or you can hold a little hot water in your mouth, then swallow it before the thermometer goes in. As for the vomit, my guess is you ran to the bathroom, made some disgusting noises and dropped vegetable beef soup in the toilet. That's pretty clever."

"I'm sick," he insists. "I can barely move."

"You're faking it, and that's okay. But you're missing a lot of school and that's not okay."

"You don't know. You're just guessing."

"Well, I know you're lying, and you shouldn't lie to your best friend."

Solve it with Hunter.
How does he know Timmy is lying?

Solution on page 80

THE DOUBLE MUGGING

It's not every kid who gets to ride along with a real cop, although crime-wise, there's very little happening in Clifton Lake. So when Mom has evening meetings, Logan and I sometimes hang out with our uncle in his patrol car.

Tonight we're strapped in the back of Officer J.B. Monroe's cruiser. We're just rolling along the closed-up shops on Main Street, windows rolled down, when Uncle J.B. hears something and stops the car. We hear it, too. It sounds like a fight. Uncle J.B. turns on his spotlight and shines it down a dark alley.

As the alley lights up, we see two men, one on the ground and the other running away. I try my best to be a detective, but all I can observe is that the running man is normal height and is wearing dark pants, a black long-sleeved top, and a cap.

"Stay here," Uncle J.B. says. Then he gets out and starts talking into the communicator on his shoulder.

Logan and I are dying to get a closer look, but we stay put until the paramedics arrive and load the man from the alley into the ambulance. As they drive off, Uncle J.B. comes back to the cruiser. "It was a mugging," he explains. "The victim had just taken cash out of an ATM. Someone came up behind him with a knife. You're never supposed to fight when someone mugs you. But he put up a fight."

"Is he going to be okay?" asks Logan.

"He's hurt, but he'll recover. The strange thing is there was another mugging. Just now. A couple of blocks from here."

"Can we go to that one?" I ask.

"Can we?" Logan chimes in. "We promise to stay in the car."

"Well, I don't have time to take you home." He mulls it over, and then starts the car.

Two minutes later, we pull up to another alley. The paramedics are already loading the second victim onto a gurney. This man is also injured with knife wounds. But he's conscious, and we lean out the window to get a better view.

The paramedics have bandaged up his lower back, where he'd been attacked, and the bandages are already soaked with blood. "I took out $200 from the cash machine," he tells Uncle J.B. "I didn't see anyone behind me. But just as I'm going down the alley, I feel this knife. 'Give me your money,' the guy says."

"Did you get a look at him?" asks Uncle J.B.

"He told me not to turn around. I handed over my wallet, and then he just stabbed me in the back. For no reason."

"So you didn't see him? You have no description?"

The man looks a little sheepish. "When he was running away, I looked around and saw him from behind. He was around my size, I guess."

"What was he wearing?"

The wounded man thinks. "He had a black sweatshirt and a Yankees baseball cap."

"That's the same guy we saw," Logan whispers.

"You can interview him later," one of the paramedics says to Uncle J.B. "We have to get him to the hospital."

Officer Monroe lets them go, and together we watch the ambulance turn on its siren and race off toward City Hospital. "What are the odds?" he asks, scratching his head. "A nice quiet town. Then we get two muggings at knife-point, within minutes."

"It's obviously the same perp," says Logan.

"Obviously," says our uncle. "If only we had a good description."

"I think I can help," I say. When there's just family

around, I don't feel so shy about speaking up. "Can you ask the officers to search around here? You know, for hiding places?"

Uncle J.B. looks puzzled. "You think the attacker is hiding out?"

"No, but I think he hid the knife. And other things. Somewhere between here and the place of the first attack."

It takes a little persuading, mostly by Logan. "If Hunter says to search the area, you should do it."

Uncle J.B. makes us stay in the cruiser. He and two other officers start searching the alley, looking in dumpsters, trash cans, and even in a garbage pile behind a restaurant. Ten minutes later, our uncle comes back to the cruiser. "Okay, boys," he says very seriously. "How did you know this?"

"What did you find?" asks Logan.

"We found a bloody knife, a dark sweatshirt, a Yankees cap, and two wallets full of money, one from each of the victims. Do you mind telling me what's going on?"

Can you solve this one?
Why did the mugger leave behind all the evidence?
What clue helped Hunter identify the mugger?

Solution on page 81

THE VANISHING PHONE

Derrick's Uncle Nigel swats at the drone, hovering right in front of him. "Get that thing out of my face!" Derrick laughs, but he uses his smart phone to maneuver the little helicopter out over the rest of his family's freakishly huge backyard. This doesn't seem to be enough for cranky Uncle Nigel, who retreats back into the house.

"I gotta be nicer to him," Derrick whispers. "Every few years, he just pops in from nowhere, hangs out around the house and spoils me rotten."

We're over at Derrick's place—Logan and me and Ginny and Martin—checking out his latest gadget. Derrick loves everything new. "The footage from the drone is going to look great on Facebook," he says. Just about everything Derrick does winds up on Facebook or Instagram, from his breakfast to the endless photos of Furrypaws, his overweight cat.

After a near-collision with a bush, Derrick lands the drone, picks it up, and leads the way into the living room. He puts his phone down on the coffee table and puts the drone squarely on top of it. Then he rubs his hands together. "I just worked up an appetite. Anyone in the mood for eats?"

In the kitchen, we all attack the fridge and cupboards. Between bites of greasy, leftover chicken, Derrick goes on and on about the drone: how expensive it was and how it instantly transmits so many gigabytes of video to his phone.

Ginny looks annoyed. She gobbles down her peanut butter and jelly sandwich. "The only time you ever have us over is when you want to show off," she snarls. Then she leaves, going through the door to the living room without even saying goodbye.

It's an awkward moment, but Derrick pretends it never

happened and starts going on about the new phone he wants to buy. "It's much cooler than the one I have, with a better camera and a bigger screen."

"Ginny's right," pipes up Martin, as he grabs the last piece of chicken. "You'd be a much nicer person if you didn't have so much stuff." And with that, Martin storms out, too.

Now it's a doubly awkward moment. But Logan and I stick by our friend...until his bragging gets too much for even us. "We should go," Logan says. Derrick follows us into the living room, still talking.

"Do you want to fly the drone?" he asks Logan. "I'll let you do it. It's easy." Derrick picks up the drone from the coffee table and then stops and makes a face. "Huh. I thought I left my phone here."

Logan and I trade puzzled looks. We distinctly remember that he did leave his phone here, under the drone, right before we went into the kitchen. I look around, and I can tell something's wrong. The pillows are on different places on the sofa. The cabinet doors and drawers are all open, and the coat closet by the front door is open.

"Huh," Derrick says again. "Maybe I left it outside."

"No," I tell him. "We all saw you put it down."

"I hate to tell you," Logan says, "but someone stole your phone."

It's funny how a normal, boring afternoon can erupt into a mystery. "I knew Ginny and Martin were jealous," says Derrick.

"Maybe they're just playing a prank," I suggest. "To get even for all the bragging."

"Is anyone else in the house?" asks Logan. "What about your uncle Nigel?"

"Uncle Nigel's a rich entrepreneur," Derrick points out. "He lives all over the world. No, it has to be Ginny or Martin. You guys are detectives. Figure it out."

Logan and I instantly turn into a couple of Sherlocks. We check the coffee table and the messed-up pillows. We examine the open cabinet and the closet. Logan's the one who discovers the tiny smear of peanut butter on the front doorknob. And I'm the one who identifies a greasy spot on the arm of a chair. It looks like chicken grease, though I can't be sure.

We're just checking under the chairs and sofa when Uncle Nigel comes downstairs. Derrick tells him what happened, and Uncle Nigel has a couple of smart questions. "Why didn't they take the drone? It's worth a lot more than the phone. Are you sure it didn't just get kicked under a table or fall behind a sofa cushion?"

"I looked everywhere," whines Derrick. "I can't do anything without a phone. I can't text or make a call, or use my drone."

"I'll buy you a new one," says Uncle Nigel, solving the problem just like that. "You've been begging your dad to get you a new phone, right?"

Derrick lights up like a Christmas tree. He tells his uncle how much the phone costs and Nigel opens his wallet and gives him more than enough cash. "I can't leave because I'm expecting a business call from Hong Kong. But you should go out and get it."

Ten seconds later Derrick is out the door, cash in his hand. We have a hard time catching up with him. "What about the crime?" Logan shouts.

"Who cares!" says Derrick. "Either I lost it or someone

pulled a prank. Well, the prank's on them." He checks his watch. "The store closes at five, so I gotta hurry."

Logan and I are left alone in the Whitfords' driveway, watching Derrick disappear down the street on his bike. "It's too bad," I say. "If he'd waited a few seconds, I could have told him what happened to his phone."

Do you know?
What happened to Derrick's phone and who is responsible?
What clues did Hunter notice?

Solution on page 82

THE CASE OF THE GHOSTLY NOTE

"We shouldn't be doing this," I tell them.

We're in the Olsen family's playroom. Timmy Olsen puts the Ouija board in the middle of the table while his older sister Gloria reads the instructions. They found the Ouija game tucked away in their attic. It's a wooden board covered with letters and numbers and weird symbols. The idea is for us to put our fingers on a rolling, pointy thing called a planchette. Then we all concentrate and try to get in touch with a spirit from the great beyond. The spirit is supposed to move the planchette and spell out a message for us.

"What's the matter?" teases Gloria. "You afraid of ghosts?"

"There are no ghosts," I say. "Someone has to push the planchette. That's the only way it can move."

"No, no. It moves by itself," says Timmy. "I've seen it on TV."

The door opens and for a second we all think it's Mrs. Olsen, coming home and catching us. But it's only our friend Sophie. "You guys ready to contact Captain McFee?" she whispers as she closes the door and turns down the lights.

Captain John McFee was the man who built the Olsens' house. One hundred years ago, the captain's boat sank in a storm. Gloria swears she's seen his ghost, all wet and slimy, roaming through the house at night. Timmy thinks maybe he's seen it, too.

This is all nonsense and will just give us bad dreams, but I don't want to be called a chicken. So I sit down with the others. We all put one finger on the planchette. Gloria takes a deep breath and begins to speak in a spooky voice. "Captain McFee, we know you're here. Please talk to us. Why are haunting this house?" Gloria watches too many horror flicks, if you ask me.

She goes on like this. And the only result is that Timmy

gets scared. "I gotta pee," he says, then runs out of the room, slamming the door behind him.

"I know your parents don't want you doing this," I say. But it's no good.

When Timmy comes back, he apologizes. He closes the door and we try again. This time the planchette starts to shake. A few seconds later it moves. I try to figure out who's pushing it.

"Are you there, Captain?" asks Sophie, her voice cracking. "Give us a sign."

The planchette moves quickly now. It takes our fingers to "t" and moves on to "h." We all spell out the words as the pointer moves from letter to letter. "This is my house," the message says. "Leave or else."

Gloria lets out a little scream. Timmy moans. "That's enough," I say. "Whoever's doing this, it's not funny."

"It's not us," says Timmy. "It's Captain McFee."

The planchette starts moving again under our fingers. "L-e-a-v-e n-o-w o-r d-i-e."

We all jump back from the table, knocking over our chairs. Gloria's hands fly up to her face. "What'll we do?"

Before I can protest again, there's a single, loud rap, like someone kicking the wall or knocking on the door. "It's the captain," shouts Sophie. "Don't let him in."

Now I'm no longer scared. I'm angry. "There's no ghost." And to prove it, I throw open the playroom door. The hallway is empty. "One of you moved the pointer," I say. "And you knocked on the wall. So just cut it out."

Gloria doesn't believe it. She runs past me into the hallway and looks around. Then she checks the other side of the playroom door. "Oh, my gosh," she gasps. "Look!"

By the time we get there, she's already pulled a note and a dangerous looking kitchen knife out of the door. "The captain left a message," she says, pointing to a gash in the middle of the wooden door.

The note is written on a piece of computer paper, with a knife hole right in the middle. "Leave this house or die!" it says in big red letters.

Timmy looks scared enough to faint. "It's blood. We have to get out of here."

"It's not blood," I say as I examine the note. "It's red crayon. And how exactly does a ghost write a note?"

"He wanted to prove to you he's real," says Sophie. "We all heard him stab the door."

"That was one of you, hitting the wall in the dark."

"What about the knife and note? You can't say that was us. We were all in the room."

"First of all, there are no ghosts." I'm talking calmly, like a condescending teacher. "One of you planned this ahead of time. Your idea of a big, unfunny joke."

I'm thinking fast and furious, trying to figure it out. Sophie, I know, was the last to arrive before the séance. Maybe she did it. But then Timmy went out to use the bathroom. And Gloria was the one who found the note.

"I know who it was," I finally tell them, "and it wasn't a ghost."

Do you know?
Who planted the knife and the note?
How did Hunter figure it out?

Solution on page 83

LOGAN'S BIG MOMENT

I've been in bed all morning. My nose is stuffed up, and I'm sneezy and achy. But the worst thing is that it's Saturday, and I can't even take off a sick day from school.

Logan drops by my room to see how I'm doing. From the start, he's being way too nice. "What do you want?" I ask. I can always tell when he wants something.

"You know Charlotte, right?" Charlotte Walker is the cutest, coolest girl in Logan's class, and he's got a crush on her. "Well, she wants me to solve a mystery. I thought you could tag along, if you don't have anything better to do."

"Anything better to do?" I can barely breathe. "You just want to impress her."

Logan doesn't deny it. "Come on. I always want you to take credit for cracking the case." He breaks into a crooked smile. "Except maybe this time."

I'm under orders to stay in bed, but we sneak out the back and make our way around the block to the Walkers' house. Charlotte meets us at the door. "You brought your little brother?" she asks, making a face. I follow Charlotte and Logan upstairs, trying not to look deathly ill. There's a sign on her door saying, "No Boys Allowed," but she lets us in anyway.

Charlotte closes her door and lowers her voice. "It's my brothers." She has three brothers. There's Noah, who's in high school. There's Charlie, who is Charlotte's twin. And there's Sebastian, who is my age, two years younger than Charlotte and Charlie. "I always keep my door locked," she says, "but one of them gets in anyway. It's driving me crazy."

"When was the last time?" asks Logan.

"This morning," says Charlotte, "right before I called you." She points to the mess of things on her dresser. "After breakfast, I came back and saw that my diary was in a different position and someone had spilled a bottle of my favorite body spray."

Logan wrinkles his nose. "What do you want me to do?"

"My parents think I'm imagining it," says Charlotte. "And my brothers just laugh. But everyone trusts you, Logan. I need you to find out who's doing it."

My brother actually blushes. "Leave it to me," he says. "Is Noah around?"

Charlotte points to Noah's room then goes downstairs while we start the investigation. Logan knocks. "What?" comes a sleepy voice that almost sounds like a grown-up's.

"Hi," my brother shouts through the door. "It's Logan, Charlotte's friend. Can I come in?"

"No. Did Charlotte send you to grill me about her privacy?" Noah laughs. "The girl's certifiable."

It's tough, questioning someone who won't even come to the door, but Logan does his best. Noah claims that he's been in his room all morning. "I had a late date last night," he says, "and I'm sleeping in. Go away."

Logan doesn't have any better luck with Charlotte's twin. Charlie's not in his room, and Logan calls him on his cell. The two of them are friends, so Logan can be a little sneakier. "Hey, Charlie?" Logan has his phone on speaker. "It's Logan. What's up? Wanna hang out?"

Even though they're twins, Charlotte and Charlie are as different as day and night. "I'm at the library," Charlie answers. He's the studious one in the family.

"The library?" Logan is skeptical. "I didn't think anyone used libraries anymore."

"Well, my computer's got a virus, and I have to do research for a paper." Charlie is half-whispering, which is believable, if he's actually in a computer cubicle in the library. According to Charlie's half-whisper, he was the first one up this morning and got to the library just when the doors opened at 8 a.m. Charlie is worried he'll get yelled at by the librarian, so he cuts the call short.

There's one last room at the end of the hallway. Sebastian, my classmate, is inside watching a video. "Hunter." He turns it off, glad to see me. Logan and I sit on his bed. I let Logan do the talking, partly because he's supposed to be the detective and partly because my head feels like it's stuffed with cotton. Sebastian is smart and he can guess why we're here. "Charlotte is so paranoid," he says. "Like any of us wants to play mind games like that. She's just doing it for attention." Then he winks at Logan. "She likes you, you know."

Like his two brothers, Sebastian has a flimsy alibi. "I was practicing the piano and then I cleaned my room." His room looks pretty clean, but then Sebastian is a bit of a neat freak.

After it's over, Logan and I retreat to Charlotte's room. Logan is beaming. "I know who did it. I'll bet you never thought I'd say that, huh?"

"What?" I'm completely thrown. "How could you know?" It's a real question. Logan and I were together for the whole investigation, yet he figured it out and I didn't. "Are you sure?"

"I'm sure," says Logan. "But don't feel bad. I have a piece of information that you don't."

What information is Logan talking about?
Which brother was in Charlotte's room?
Why did Hunter miss the clue?

Solution on page 84

THE MYSTERY OF THE ROSES

I am not one of the cool kids. But it's still nice when Quincy Neustrom wants to hang out with me after school. Sure, Logan is just as cool, but he's my brother, so it doesn't count.

The day has warmed up a lot, and we stuff our jackets in our backpacks before starting to throw around a Frisbee. "Logan brags about you," Quincy shouts. The park is nearly empty, but it's still kind of embarrassing to hear. "He says you're the brains behind all the mysteries he's been solving."

I'm not sure if Quincy is praising or teasing me. Either way, I miss the next catch. The Frisbee sails up behind my head, grabs a breeze, and gets lodged in the branches of a huge maple at the far end of the park, right by a tall fence. "Sorry," I shout, even more embarrassed.

I race over to the tree. But before I can do anything, Quincy is there, clambering up the trunk like a cat. He balances on one leg, grabs the Frisbee, then glances down into the neighbor's yard on the other side of the fence. "Holy…" Even from twenty feet away, I can see his eyes go wide.

"What's wrong?" I ask.

"It's Ms. Finkelton's yard," he shouts. Of course I know it's Ms. Finkelton's yard. Everyone around the park knows fussy Ms. Finkelton. She's always complaining about the noise and the balls flying into her yard. "Someone cut the roses off her bushes. They're all around the lawn in a big mess. You think maybe she did it herself?"

"I truly doubt that," I say. The woman is famous for her gardens. "What do you think we should do?"

"You have to investigate." Quincy's words sound like a dare, and almost without thinking, I agree. It takes me only a minute to run out of the park, around the corner, and around the next corner to Ms. Finkelton's street. The front of her house is easy to spot. It's got colorful flowers and bushes everywhere, all perfectly trimmed.

"Hello?" I ring the doorbell and look through the windows. I try waiting patiently, until I'm just about to give up. And then Ms. Finkelton arrives, coming home from her daily walk to the garden center. "Hunter Monroe?" She puts her bag of mulch down on the porch. "Can I help you?"

I try explaining what Quincy saw. But she doesn't believe me until Quincy comes around the corner, wearing his jacket and carrying both of our backpacks. Then Ms. Finkelton leads the way through the house, into the backyard. We all see it at the same time—her prized rose bushes, vandalized, the red and white roses tossed around the manicured lawn.

Ms. Finkelton almost faints. "Why would they do this? I know the little monsters don't like me, but this is pure evil."

"Who doesn't like you?" I ask.

It turns out that the Finkelton niece and nephew, Angela and Adam, are in the house, visiting for a few hours while their parents are at an appointment. Adam has been in the basement playing video games, while Angela has been in her aunt's bedroom upstairs, watching a DVR. The kids are both younger than me, still in grade school. They act annoyed at being interrupted and brought to the backyard, even when Ms. Finkelton shows them what happened.

"Don't look at me," says Adam. "I haven't been in the yard since we got here."

Angela says, "I opened the back door to let the cat out. Maybe fifteen minutes ago. I didn't notice anything."

"So it happened in the last fifteen minutes," I say.

"I go to the garden center every day at this time," says Ms. Finkelton. "I thought they would be fine here by themselves. Apparently, I was wrong."

Quincy eyes me closely, expecting me to be a detective. I do my best. I pretend to be interested in Adam's video game, following him down to the basement. I try on his headphones just as he takes the game off pause. The battle noise is deafening. But I keep my cool, checking around for any stray rose petals or scissors he could have used.

When I get up to Ms. Finkelton's bedroom, I see the movie Angela was watching. It's also on pause. Again, I find no rose petals. But there's a pair of fabric scissors in her aunt's sewing kit.

Next, Quincy and Ms. Finkelton come out to the backyard with me, the scene of the crime. "I don't suppose it could be the cat," says Quincy.

Ms. Finkelton says Gaston would never ruin her roses. And when I check the roses, I agree. The stems have been snipped cleanly. "Do you have a pair of clippers?"

"You mean pruning shears?" Ms. Finkelton goes into her garden shed and points to a small pair of heavy-duty clippers. The blades look perfectly clean and dry, like they hadn't been used in a while.

I ask Ms. Finkelton if she has any other pruning shears. "No, and the only other scissors in the house are the fabric scissors, nail scissors, and a dull pair of kitchen scissors.

"Do Adam and Angela know the pruning shears are here?" I ask.

"I often make them help with the gardening," says Ms. Finkelton. "So, yes, they know."

I continue to examine the yard and the thorny row of rosebushes. I study several rose flowers, all of them snipped by a sharp blade. And all the while, Quincy watches me, hands stuffed in his jacket pockets, waiting for me to solve the mystery.

Can you help Hunter out?
Who snipped off the roses?
What clues point to the rose vandal?

Solution on page 85

"Someone chopped down Old Gnarly!" Timmy is almost crying. Old Gnarly was our favorite, an oak tree that we've been climbing up and playing in all our lives. When Timmy and I rode over on our bikes today, it was on the ground, with the sawdust from a chainsaw all over the grass and road. "Who would want to kill Old Gnarly?"

"I can think of three people," I say right off the top of my head.

Old Gnarly has been entertaining young pirates and Robin Hoods for maybe a hundred years. Then someone bought the land all around it and built three houses that faced the tree in a tight, little semicircle. Almost instantly, the homeowners began complaining, trying to get the tree removed, as if they just realized it was there. In a typical summer like this, the huge leaves almost completely block their second-floor windows.

"You're right. They're the only ones with a motive." Timmy's my best friend, and I guess he's starting to think like me. "Let's figure this out and have them arrested."

It's a scary thought, confronting grownups without some sort of backup. Lucky for me, a police cruiser pulls up and my uncle, Officer J.B. Monroe jumps out. "Someone chopped down Big Boy," he shouts, looking just as crushed as Timmy. It turns out that J.B. also played here. He and his friends even built a treehouse, until their parents made them take it down.

I tell him about my suspicions. "It's against the law, right? You can't cut an old tree without city permission."

Uncle J.B. confirms this. "It's a huge fine. Come on. Let's talk to them." And just like that, Timmy and I are part of a police investigation.

Mr. Jim Taylor owns the house on the left. He answers the door and instantly knows why we're here. "I didn't do it," he says. "I drove up fifteen minutes ago and the tree was already down."

"Do you own a chainsaw?" my uncle asks.

The man admits to having a chainsaw, but he refuses to let my uncle inspect it. Not without a warrant, he says. As we're leaving his property, I take a peek at his car, and I notice a few bits of sawdust embedded in the tire treads.

When we approach the house in the middle, the owner, Ms. Elway, is already on her porch. Inside, we can hear a couple of dogs, barking away. She's a large, athletic woman and seems amused by the sight of us. "What is this, bring-your-kid-to-work day?"

"These are my deputies," Uncle J.B. says. It's a joke, but Timmy and I both stand a little taller.

Ms. Elway also denies cutting down the tree. "I was out walking my dogs on the trails behind my house. I heard the chainsaw from a distance, but I didn't think anything of it. Whoever cut it down is a hero in my book. Now I finally have a view."

Ms. Elway admits to owning a chainsaw and invites us into her garage. From where I stand, the chainsaw looks clean, almost brand new. But then everything in the garage looks that way. It's the cleanest garage I've ever seen.

At the third house, the one closest to the tree, there's a car in the driveway, its path blocked by a huge limb from the fallen oak. When my uncle rings the bell, there's no answer. He rings again. "Door's open," comes a man's voice from upstairs. "Who is it?"

"It's the police," says Officer Monroe. "Can we come in?"

The voice tells us to come upstairs. As soon as we walk into the room, Timmy and I recognize it. This is the bedroom we could look into from the tree branches. On more than one occasion, we accidentally saw the owner exercising on a treadmill in front of the window. We always scrambled out of sight to another branch.

The man is at a desk in the corner. He gets up and introduces himself—Kevin Eversol, a banker who's been working from home. "You're the kids in the tree," he says. Timmy and I are super embarrassed. "Well, I'm sorry someone cut it down. But I have no idea who."

"But your car is blocked in," says Uncle J.B., "which means you were here when it happened. You must have seen something."

Mr. Eversol appears thrown, but he recovers. "I was in the basement, looking through some old files. I heard the chainsaw and assumed it was one of my neighbors who finally snapped. To be honest, I didn't want to know."

"Both of your neighbors say they weren't here when it happened," my uncle points out. "That leaves only you."

"That's not true," says Mr. Eversol, pointing to the window. "I was on the treadmill this morning. I saw Jim Taylor in his garage. Carla Elway was home, too. I saw her walking her dogs out front."

Uncle J.B. asks Mr. Eversol if he has a chainsaw. He says he doesn't, but then he refuses to let us check his garage and asks us to leave. We step outside just as the Parks Department truck pulls up. From the anguished reaction of the supervisor, it looks he has fond memories of Old Gnarly, too.

"I think they all did it," Timmy whispers.

"It could be," says my uncle. "Or it could be a total stranger. We have no proof."

"Well, one of them lied to us," I say. "So that person is probably guilty of something."

Can you ID the liar?
Who gave a false statement?
How does Hunter know it's a lie?

Solution on page 86

A CASE OF THE SPARKLES

Call it my sixth sense, but I can always tell when there's a mystery. This morning, for example, I'm walking into the band room when I see my brother and our friend Jocelyn in a corner, talking seriously. She runs a hand through her hair, glancing around as the other kids take out their instruments. Logan sees me and gives me that "come here" look. Definitely a mystery.

"Hey, Jocelyn," I say, trying to seem mature and casual. "I like the sparkles."

Jocelyn rolls her eyes. "Not funny, Hunter." She touches her hair again and a few glittery stars fall out, one of them sticking to the tip of her nose. She blows it off.

"Someone's been throwing glitter on Joss's head," says Logan.

"Who did it?" I ask.

"I don't know," she answers. "Someone pointed it out during first period."

I'm puzzled. "How could you not notice someone throwing glitter on you?" Jocelyn is the tallest kid in school, with her hair swooped up on top. It would take luck and a great pitching arm to get glitter up there without being noticed.

"And this isn't the first time," Logan says. "Someone did it last week, right? I saw it on your shoulders, but I thought it might be a fashion statement."

"So embarrassing." Jocelyn's face turns red. "It's actually the third time this month."

"Three times? And you never noticed?" I ask. That is a mystery. "Any idea who would want to do this?" One suspect comes to mind. "How about Tony?"

Everyone knows that Jocelyn and Tony, her little brother, don't get along. He's a lot shorter and she makes fun of him and he makes fun of her, which is the way most brothers and sisters act, I guess.

"I wish it was that little nerd." Jocelyn snarls and punches her fist into her hand. "But I always check my hair when I leave the house. And the two of us don't walk to school together. And we don't share any classes, so I don't see how he could be the one."

"What about the kids who sit behind you?" This is Logan's idea and it's a good one. "You're a lot shorter when you sit down. All they'd have to do is lean forward."

Jocelyn thinks. "Fiona Albright is behind me in homeroom. But Fiona's a friend. She's always whispering jokes in my ear and cracking me up."

"Sounds like a perfect way to get glitter in your hair," I suggest, "when you're distracted like that."

Jocelyn looks disappointed at the thought. Fiona Albright is pretty and popular and pretends to like everyone, even unimportant little me. "It could also be Hugo Green," Jocelyn says. "He sits behind me in first period. He's the one who pointed out the glitter."

"Is there any reason Hugo would do it?" Logan asks.

"No," says Jocelyn. "Hugo likes me…a lot."

"Maybe he likes you too much." Logan lowers his voice. "I've seen Hugo waiting for you in the hallway between classes. I've also seen you avoiding him."

"I don't avoid him," she hisses back. "I just don't want a boyfriend, okay?"

It's a good thing they're whispering because just now, as they're discussing Fiona and Hugo, the two suspects walk in, looking like best friends. "Hey, Logan," says Hugo. "Hey, Joss." Hugo is almost as tall as Jocelyn and spends most of his time thinking about girls. "Fiona and I were just discussing your sparkly hair."

Fiona laughs, like it's the funniest thing ever. "Don't you love it? Joss does this all the time, like she's still in grade school."

"Not all the time," Jocelyn shoots back. "I mean, I don't do it. Someone else does." This strikes Fiona and Hugo as even funnier, and they laugh all the way to their chairs in the clarinet section.

"Ugh." Jocelyn scratches through her hair, trying once and for all to get rid of the glitter.

"Your hair's a little wet." Logan picks a sparkle from her shoulders. "That's why it's sticking."

"It's like this every time," Jocelyn moans. "Every time."

"What do you mean?" I ask, my detective senses going on high alert.

She sighs, like I'm the world's dumbest kid. "I mean it was raining this morning. And it was raining last week when it happened."

"So, someone throws glitter on you when it rains?" I ask. "Only when you come to school in the rain?"

"I don't know." She sighs again. "I guess."

Logan must also have a sixth sense, because he knows that I just solved the mystery.

Are you as smart as Hunter?
Who put the glitter in Jocelyn's hair?
How did the culprit do it?

Solution on page 87

THE OLD TEAPOT

It's Saturday morning. Logan and I are walking down Main Street after a winter storm, enjoying how our shoes make footprints in the layer of new snow. Up ahead, someone else is making snowy prints, pacing back and forth to a little side alley. Ms. Culpepper, one of our gym teachers, sees us and races over, looking all nervous.

"I don't know what to do." She points to the shabby, one-story building on the corner of Main and the alley. "I think someone broke into that store." Then she walks us into the alley, and I see what she's talking about. The old skylight on the slanted roof looks broken, like someone pried it up. We can also see footprints going up the fire escape of the next-door building and over to the skylight.

"Who would want to rob that place?" Logan asks, making a face. My brother has a point. This is Al's Emporium, a run-down, dusty store full of cheap odds and ends. A lot of places like this get spruced up and call themselves antique shops. But Al Simmons is too old and cranky for that.

"Hey. What are you doing?" We all turn and see cranky Mr. Simmons himself, getting out of his truck and coming our way.

Ms. Culpepper explains the situation. Then we follow Mr. Simmons around to Main Street, where he unlocks the door and lets us in. Right away I notice the wet footprints. They start on the floor, under the skylight, and head around to the cash register. Mr. Simmons checks the drawer. "I had about a hundred bucks in here. Now it's gone."

"We shouldn't touch anything," I say. "Not until the police come."

Logan is just about to call our uncle, the cop, when someone else walks in. "Excuse me." It's a man I half recognize from around town. He's rubbing his hands together, trying to warm them up. "Hello?"

"You again," Mr. Simmons shouts. "Get out."

But the man doesn't leave. "I was hoping you had changed your mind about the teapot."

"Nope. Not for sale. Not at the price you're offering." And with that, Al Simmons goes to the front display window. He's looking for the teapot. But among all the dusty knickknacks is an empty space, right in the middle. "It's gone," he gasps. "The thief took the only thing worth taking."

"So, you don't have it anymore?" asks the man.

The shop owner throws him a look that could kill a horse, and the man retreats, stopping only to pick up his gloves off the front counter before fleeing out the door.

"Serves you right, Al," Ms. Culpepper smirks. "That was my teapot and you know it."

"Hmph," snorts Mr. Simmons. "I paid you two bucks for it. Fair and square."

"It was not fair," she answers. "You knew it was valuable, and you cheated me."

From what I can piece together, Ms. Culpepper sold Mr. Simmons a lot of junk from her mother's garage. One of the things in the junk was an old, flowery teapot. When Mr. Simmons looked it up online, the teapot turned out to be an antique. An appraiser had come by to confirm it. He could get at least $5,000. For a teapot!

"It was you." Mr. Simmons points a gnarly finger at the gym teacher. "You broke in and made it look like a regular robbery, just to get it back."

Ms. Culpepper stammers. "That's a lie. I'll bet you stole it yourself."

"Why would I do that?"

"Insurance," says Ms. Culpepper. "As soon as the appraiser gave you a written valuation, the teapot was covered. You could steal it, get the insurance money, and then sell it secretly."

"Don't you have an alarm system?" asks Logan. "Or cameras? How about locks?"

Mr. Simmons shakes his head. "There was never much worth stealing. But the front door locks automatically, even when I forget."

This isn't quite true. Logan tries the door and discovers that it only locks automatically from the outside. "My guess is the thief got in through the skylight," he deduces. "Then he—or she—left by the front door, which was a lot easier than climbing back up to the skylight. You didn't use the deadbolt last night, Mr. Simmons, did you?"

The shop owner shrugs. "Maybe I forgot."

As Mr. Simmons and Ms. Culpepper keep arguing, Logan and I circle the dusty shop. From the lack of melted snow on the floor, we figure the skylight must have been pried opened after the snow stopped falling, which was maybe half an hour ago. The evaporating shoe prints are medium sized and could belong to just about any adult, male or female. "It could be the customer, too," I say. "He obviously knew the teapot was valuable."

"Then why did he come back just now?" Logan asks. "If he'd already stolen it…"

There are a lot of things to mull over: the timing of the theft, the athletic ability of the thief, the weather. But by the time our uncle, Officer J.B. Monroe, shows up, I have the mystery solved.

Did you figure it out?
Which suspect stole the teapot?
What was the clue Hunter spotted?

Solution on page 88

TWO PERFECT ALIBIS

I'm in social studies class, daydreaming about nothing, when my brother knocks on the door and tells Mrs. Denning that the principal wants to see me. Being called to the principal's office isn't that unusual for Logan and me, since Mom's the principal.

"We got a mystery," he whispers as we hurry down the hall. The two of us have solved more than a few head-scratching puzzles.

"Hunter." When we walk into her outer office, Mom is surprised to see me. "I didn't ask Logan to bring you, but it's good. The more brains, the better." She glances toward the closed door to her inner office and lowers her voice. "Some students have been smoking on school property. We don't know how many. But when Coach Iverson went into the equipment room today around 12:30 this afternoon, he smelled the smoke. He also found cigarette butts and matches."

"I know the equipment room is kept locked," Logan says. "Do any kids have keys to it?"

"Two of them do," Mom whispers, glancing again at her inner door. "Jeremy Hall is equipment manager for the football team. And Brenda Buxby is manager of the field hockey team. I don't like to think of either of them smoking, especially in school."

"What do you want us to do?" I ask. I hope she doesn't ask us to interrogate Jeremy and Brenda. That would be so awkward. But it doesn't seem necessary, since both of them have alibis.

Mom explains. "We have a witness, someone in the fitness room next to the equipment room. He says he definitely heard people in there at 11:55 a.m. Exactly, he says. But at 11:55,

Jeremy was talking to a teacher after math class. Around noon, he says he used the boys' room, then met up with his friends in the cafeteria."

"So he's in the clear for 11:55," Logan says. "What about Brenda?"

"Brenda and her friends were in the cafeteria, too. Coach Iverson says he saw them there, from about 11:45 to 12:15."

"What about the witness?" I ask. "The kid in the fitness room. Maybe he's the smoker."

"I don't think so," Mom says. "First of all, that student doesn't have a key to the equipment room. And second, it was Sonny Maddox."

Everyone in school knows Sonny. He's captain of the football team and the most health-crazy kid. If Sonny catches you eating a candy bar or a doughnut, you're in for a lecture.

"Jeremy and Brenda are in my office," Mom says. "I'm going to keep questioning them. But I'd like for you to talk to Sonny."

Mom gives us both hall passes, and we soon track down Sonny. He's in the fitness room, as usual. It's his home away from home.

The fitness room looks like a typical gym, with a couple of rowing machines, stationary bikes, and exercise mats. There are also a few weight machines facing a wall of mirrors, so you can watch yourself work out.

Sonny is on a rowing machine when we walk in. "Logan. I'll bet your mom sent you, right?" Logan is already famous for solving things.

"Yeah," Logan admits. "It's kind of a puzzle, don't you think?"

"Hey, I know what I saw," Sonny says, a little defensively. "I was on the bench press." He points to one of the weight machines facing the mirror. "When I heard the noise from the equipment room, I looked up and checked the clock. It was five minutes to twelve. I went back to my routine and lost track of the time. I wound up late for my next class."

I look at the clock on the wall above the door and compare it to my watch. The time matches exactly.

"Did you see anyone or recognize any voices?" Logan asks.

"Nope," says Sonny. "They got in through the hallway door. I'd tell you if I knew anything more. Have you ever seen pictures of a smoker's lung? Gross."

The older boys talk for another minute, but I stop listening. I already know what must have happened. When we get back out in the hall, Logan breaks into a grin. "You know who did it, don't you?"

I never get tired of him saying that.

Can you break one of the alibis?
Who smoked in the equipment room?
What clue did Hunter notice?

Solution on page 89

BAND ROOM REVENGE

"Who did this?"

All the band members are glancing around at the graffiti. It's spray painted everywhere—all the walls and the ceiling, in three different colors. But even worse than the paint is what the paint spells out. Every tag is an insult to Mr. Anthony Ashton, our band director. They range from "Worst Teacher Ever" and "Tone-deaf Tony", to others that weren't as clever and definitely ruder. Mr. Ashton is all red in the face. "Does anyone know who did this?"

For once, I don't have a clue. Yesterday after school we practiced on the field, and Mr. Ashton, who is usually an okay guy, yelled at us for an hour. Nothing we did was right. He even yelled at Logan, who's first trumpet and hardly ever makes a mistake.

"All right," Mr. Ashton says. "You give me no choice. You're going to spend every class cleaning this up, all of you. No rehearsals. And no trip to Burlingate High. I'm canceling it."

All of us are stunned. It isn't fair. We've been looking forward to our bus trip and our overnight stay and especially to playing during halftime at a high school football game. It's all we've been talking about.

Mr. Ashton hands out the cleaners, brushes, and pails, and then walks out, leaving us to grumble and scrub. Meanwhile, Logan comes up to me. "Let's go talk to Mom."

Mom is in her office and she instantly knows why we came. "Don't even argue," she says. "Mr. Ashton is just as disappointed as you. He used to teach at Burlingate. When I first told him about the trip, he was so excited."

"We know," says Logan, rolling his eyes. "He told us a million times, how they had the best band in the state, and how he wrote the march they play at all the games."

Mom ignores his sarcasm. "If the guilty party comes forward and confesses, then maybe you can go. If not, I think it's a fair punishment."

Logan and I head back to the band room. Along the way, we bump into Mr. Turnabene, the custodian. He can tell by our faces exactly what's going on. "In trouble for the graffiti, huh? Well, it's pretty bad stuff. When I first laid eyes on it yesterday…"

"Did you discover it?" I ask, already treating this like an investigation.

"I did," he says. "Maybe half an hour after band practice. I was repairing a sprinkler pipe in the basement when the alarm went off."

"The band room has an alarm?" I ask. This is news.

"I knew that," says Logan. "Once you open the door, you have thirty seconds before it goes off."

Mr. Turnabene nods. "Some valuable instruments are stored there. When the alarm went off, I ran up to see. Couldn't have been more than two minutes. Someone had broken the door lock and already trashed the place. Your mom got there about the same time. She turned off the alarm."

"Don't you have the alarm code?" Logan asks.

"Nah. As far as I know, it's just your mom and Mr. Ashton."

"Was anything missing from the band room?" I ask.

"Mr. Ashton and your mom checked it out. Nothing was touched—except for all the paint."

We thank Mr. Turnabene, and then join the others. Jocelyn is standing on a stool in the middle of the room, scrubbing the ceiling. She's the tallest kid in school, so all she needs is a stool. "Hey, get to work," she shouts at us. "This is going to take forever."

"It's not fair," says Ginny. "Some jerks spend ten minutes making this mess, and it'll take us days to fix it."

"Can't we just pay someone to repaint?" says Derrick. Derrick's parents are rich and he thinks money can solve everything.

There's no scrub brush left for me, so I look around. That's when I notice that all the graffiti is in the same hand-writing. The "T"s all have the same type of cross-stroke. And the "H"s have the same loop at the top. I go over to Logan who's been attacking a red streak by the window. He sees me and stops. "I think I know who did it," I whisper. "But it doesn't make sense."

Logan makes sure no one else is within earshot, and then listens as I talk about the identical handwriting and the alarm system. At the end, he's as puzzled as I am. But he knows I'm right.

Can you match Hunter's brain power?
Who did the vandalism?
What is the clue about the alarm system?

Solution on page 89

THE UNLOCKED BIKE

It's a miserable, cold Saturday, with rain showers coming and going. But it's a perfect day for an indoor birthday party. The birthday boy is Derrick Whitford, so it's a big bash with a ton of kids, games, music…and food. Derrick likes his food.

Logan is much more of a party animal, so he takes along our present and gets there early. By the time I work up the courage, it's midafternoon. In the Whitfords' front hall, I slither out of my rain slicker and hang it up on top of the other few dozen soggy coats balancing themselves on the five or six hooks.

Right away I see my brother. "About time," he shouts over the music. "You're the last one." Barely a second later and he's proven wrong. The door bangs open and Casey Black stumbles in. Behind him, the skies suddenly open up. This new downpour looks like it may be around for a while.

Casey is a big, messy, forgetful kid. "Lucky me," he says, taking off his helmet and coat. "I wanted to ride my new bike. Looks like I barely made it." He points to a green mountain bike with chunky tires, propped up against a tree by the curb.

"Is that my present?" Derrick has just finished a handful of chips and is licking the grease from his fingers.

"It's not your present," Casey laughs. "I forgot your present."

"That's okay," says Derrick. "I'll take the bike."

"Is that a Kiwi L-300?" asks Wanda Dee. Wanda seems to know every brand name in the world. "Ooh, they're like super rare. Sold out everywhere."

It's just the five of us by the door, staring out at the cool bike in the rain. "Did you lock it up?" asks Logan.

Casey shakes his head. "I was too focused on getting inside." Logan tries to convince him to go out and lock it around the tree, but Casey isn't worried. "No one's going to walk by in this mess and steal a bike." He leaves it like that and closes the door.

It turns out to be a pretty great party, taking up the whole first floor of the huge house. For once I don't hang around my brother like some puppy. I actually relax and play a few games. I spend some time talking to Wanda, but then she disappears. Derrick loves his presents, but when his mom stops bringing out more food, he gets pouty and goes up to his room.

The party's still going strong. No one seems to have left. And then Casey wants to show off his new bike. Logan and I are in the front room, not far away, when Casey opens the door and lets out a scream. His bike is no longer by the tree. It's gone.

The rain is still coming down, so I grab my slicker. Logan grabs his from the top of the hook next to mine. Casey doesn't grab anything, but leads the way out to the curb. It's just the three of us, with an audience of curious partiers hanging around the dry doorway. Logan and I have our hoods up, but Casey is getting soaked. "How could I be so stupid?"

"I told you to lock it up," says Logan.

"I thought it would be safe. On a day like today? Who would even drive by and see it wasn't locked?"

"Maybe it wasn't someone driving by," I suggest. "Maybe it was someone from the party."

"From the party?" Logan looks concerned. "What makes you say that?"

"Well, as soon as Casey got here, he let several people know that he had a great new bike and that it wasn't locked."

"Yeah," says Casey, glancing back at the house. "Derrick

said it should be his present and Wanda really seemed to want it."

"That's right," I say. "Anyone could have left the party, taken the bike, and hidden it somewhere."

"You talk like you know who it was," says Casey.

"I think I do." Then I take poor, water-logged Casey by the arm and point him toward the house. "I'll explain when we get inside."

Do you know who it was?
Who stole Casey's bike?
What clue tipped Hunter off?

Solution on page 91

SCIENCE FAIR SABOTAGE

"I could go all the way to the nationals with this," boasts Nicholas Barker. Nicholas thinks he's easily the smartest kid in our school. And he's right.

It's Friday after school. Timmy, Gloria, and I are with Nicholas in his garage, looking at the science fair project that he says will make him famous. It's full of battery parts and wires and coils and diagrams.

"It's a breakthrough," he tells us. "A way to make an ordinary battery last almost twice as long. I bet I can sell this to a big company and make millions."

Nicholas may be brilliant, but Timmy, Gloria, and I don't believe his claim. But we're still jealous. Timmy has worked hard on his own science project, "The Aerodynamics of Skee-Ball." Gloria has a display on the respiration of goldfish, and I've been spending weeks on "Fingerprints and DNA." Tomorrow is Saturday, when we all set up in the school auditorium. Nicholas's entry will probably blow everything else's away.

"I just need to make a few adjustments," Nicholas says. "Would you guys mind taking out the trash? The garbage truck comes early on Saturdays—by 7:00 a.m.—and my Dad screams if I forget to put it out. Thanks."

Gloria is insulted by this, and she leaves without saying a word. But Timmy and I do as we're told, wheeling the heavy plastic bin out to the curb. "I'd like to smash his stupid battery to pieces," Timmy hisses. Then he slumps down the street toward his house, and I slump off toward mine.

It's about eight the next morning when Nicholas pounds on my front door. I put down my cereal bowl and meet him outside. "Did you sabotage me?" he shouts. "Did you steal my project?"

My brother and Mom are still in bed, so I lead him away from the house. "I didn't steal anything. What are you talking about?"

As we walk the two blocks to his house, Nicholas accuses me again. "Where were you around eleven last night?"

"I was asleep in bed. Why?"

"Someone got into the garage," he says. "My room is right above. I heard a noise, like glass breaking. I checked the clock. But I was half asleep, and I thought it must be a raccoon. This morning I walked into the garage and it was gone. The Battery Life Extender was gone."

When we get to his house, I can see a broken pane of glass in the garage's walk-through door. Someone broke the glass, reached inside, and unlocked the knob. I look over to the workbench, and sure enough, Nicholas's project is no longer there. "When did you last see it?"

"Around nine last night," he says. "I did one final check, and it worked perfectly. I should have got up when I heard the noise, but I didn't think you'd be jealous enough to do this."

"I didn't. Maybe someone's pulling a prank." Nicholas wants to call the police, but I manage to calm him down. "Maybe the judges will give you an extra week."

"I can't start over from scratch," says Nicholas. "I can't."

"What if I find it?" I ask. It would have been hard for the thief to take the battery extender very far. So I go out to the curb and look inside the Barkers' garbage bin. "Here it is!" I point to the mass of broken coils and snipped wires and torn-up diagrams nestled in the otherwise empty bin. "I can help you put it back together."

We turn the bin over and try to reconstruct it right there

on the sidewalk. "Impossible." Nicholas is almost crying. "It's a delicate machine. There's no way."

Nicholas starts throwing everything back in the trash when a large SUV stops at the curb. It's Mr. Olsen, driving Timmy and Gloria to school to set up their projects. "Hey, boys. What's wrong?"

Nicholas explains what happened last night while I keep my eye on Timmy and Gloria, who are not looking all that upset. "I was in my room, working with my goldfish," Gloria volunteers, without even being asked.

"I was going to talk to you about that, young lady," says Mr. Olsen. "It must have been nearly midnight when I saw your light go out. That's not acceptable."

"Well, what about Timmy?" asks Gloria. Her brother punches her on the shoulder. She ignores the punch and keeps talking. "I heard him in the basement, working on that Skee-Ball thing—after he promised you he was going to bed."

"So you were both up at 11:00 p.m.?" asks Nicholas, suddenly alert and focused. "Did anyone else see you? Gloria could have climbed out of her window and onto the trellis. And Timmy could have slipped out of the basement door without being seen. Either one of you."

It's kind of funny, watching Nicholas insult his friends and pretend to be a sleuth. He's not even asking the right questions.

As for me, I already know who did it.

Do you know?
Who wrecked Nicholas's project?
What clue did Hunter notice?

Solution on page 92

67

THE CASE OF THE STOLEN DIAMOND

Our neighbor Mrs. Lake is sick, so I'm taking her dog, Rufus, for a walk. Tonight is one of those perfectly quiet nights. A female jogger is the only person we see or hear—until an ear-piercing car alarm makes Rufus and me jump. It sounds like it's right around the corner. I'm in the process of picking up the little poodle's poo, so it takes half a minute for me to go take a look.

When we turn the corner, I see a young man come out of his house and walk over to the steady blare of the BMW parked across the street. He's angry, probably thinking it's a false alarm. By this time Rufus is spooked, so I take him back to our block and then home to Mrs. Lake. Eventually the alarm stops.

I'm just settling down to the last of my homework when I see flashing lights through the window, blue and white, like a police cruiser. I shout out to Mom that I'll be back soon. Then I race out the door.

I've heard plenty of car alarms, but this is the first time I've seen a car break-in. My uncle, Officer J.B. Monroe, is in his uniform, standing by the smashed glass of the front passenger window. He's talking to the man I saw crossing the street toward the car earlier. The man's a lot calmer now. "My name's Randy Smith. I was on my way over to Chet's to yell at him for his stupid alarm. When I saw the broken window, I went and knocked on his door."

"Did you touch anything?" asks Officer Monroe. Randy shakes his head. "Did you see anyone else on the street?"

"No one," he says, which makes sense since Rufus and I had been a good twenty yards away and it was pretty dark. "Well, Annabelle from the next block…she's usually out jogging at this hour, but I didn't see her."

"Annabelle Lewis?" asks the other man at the scene. "She's Julia's best friend. You think Annabelle could have done this?" This other man seems to be the victim, the owner of the BMW with the smashed window. I listen carefully, piecing together as much as I can.

His name is Chet Galinski—at least it sounds like Galinski. He's tall and good looking and his house is one of the new McMansions that are popping up in the area. He says he was at a fancy restaurant tonight, where he proposed to his girlfriend, a woman named Julia. And Julia said "no."

"It was a two-carat diamond," he tells the officer. "I was really upset. Imagine her turning me down! When I got home I guess I just left the ring box on the passenger seat."

"On the front seat?" asks Uncle J.B. "A fancy ring box in plain sight? Under a streetlight?" He sighs. "For how long?"

"I got home maybe an hour ago," says Chet. "I went straight to my den at the back of the house, put on some jazz, and poured myself a drink."

Uncle J.B. writes it all down. "Did you hear your car alarm go off?"

"I guess," says Chet. "But I didn't think it could be an actual break-in."

"Is the ring insured?"

Chet shakes his head. "I was going to return it to the jeweler, but now I can't." He groans. "Plus I need to get my BMW repaired."

A moment later, another person comes along. It's Annabelle Lewis, the jogger I had seen when I was out with Rufus. She's walking now and breathing heavy, taking the earbuds out of her ears. "Chet?" she says to the one man. "Randy?"

70

she says to the other. She sees the police car and the broken window. "Officer? What's going on?"

My uncle explains the situation, including Chet's rejected proposal. Annabelle thinks this is funny. "I kept telling Julia not to trust you. It must have finally sunk in. Serves you right."

It seems that Chet had dated Annabelle for a while, then called it off and started dating her best friend, Julia. This sounds to me like a motive to steal Chet's engagement ring. Uncle J.B. thinks so, too. "You were jogging along this block tonight?" he asks Annabelle. "Did you see Mr. Galinski's car?"

"I run this route every night," Annabelle says. "I suppose I saw the BMW."

"Did you look inside?"

"No, I didn't. I did hear the alarm. But you hear car alarms all the time around here."

Uncle J.B. has one more question. He turns to the neighbor. "Mr. Smith," he says, "how long was it from the time the alarm started to the time you came outside?"

"Maybe thirty seconds," says Randy Smith. "Whoever smashed the window and took the ring was already gone."

"Hi, Uncle J.B." I step up to the car and hear the crunch of glass under my feet. In the front passenger seat, I see a rock nestled in the shattered glass. It perfectly matches the other rocks in Chet Galinski's garden. It would have taken just a few seconds to break the window and snatch the ring box. "I think I'm a witness."

"Hunter?" My uncle is surprised to see me. "Did you see what happened?"

"No, sir," I say. "I was walking Mrs. Lake's dog. I saw the same things Mr. Smith did. But…"

Before I can go on, Uncle J.B. takes me aside. "Don't say anything in front of the suspects."

He's right. Because I already know who the thief is.

Are you as smart as Hunter?
Who broke the window and stole the diamond?
How does Hunter know?

Solution on page 93

HUNTER AND THE BLUE CANOE

Our week at Camp Winitaka always starts the same. On the first day, the kids flock to the meeting hall, all excited to see each other. Then we divide into teams for the Camp Games, our big competition of the week.

I'm not good at sports. I can barely catch a ball. But last year I somehow won the boys' solo canoe race for the Blue Team, in the under-13 division. I'm hoping to win again, so I grab a blue T-shirt from my team's pile. Logan usually wins three or four events, but he isn't here this year. So it's up to me, trying to uphold the family reputation.

"I'm going to blow you away, Monroe." This is Kent Tillis, a born bully. "Like you're standing still." He's grown a lot since last year, and he takes a large red T-shirt from the Red Team's pile.

"Last year was a fluke," taunts Buster with a smirk. Buster Hennessy hasn't grown at all. The wiry kid can still fit into a size small T-shirt. He finds the very last one in the Green Team's pile of shirts and changes into it before one of the smaller girls can claim it.

The counselors put the leftover shirts back on a shelf and then announce the schedule. The boys' canoe race will be first thing tomorrow, before any of us even have time to practice. I'm tempted to take out a canoe after dinner. The boatshed is never locked. But the staff just painted the building, and there's a big "Wet Paint—Keep Out" sign on the door.

The canoes are out on the beach when we get there the next morning. The Blue Team is out in force, cheering me on. The racers are me, Kent, Buster, Woody, and a new camper playing for the Yellow Team. He's big and looks like a huge, pumped-up banana, glaring at little me, the defending champ.

At the whistle, we're supposed to run to our canoes, carry them into the lake, then paddle around a floating marker and back to shore. I get a good start and run straight for the canoe with the blue flag. Ten seconds later, I'm in the water, stroking as hard as I can. But I'm not picking up speed. Something's wrong.

I feel it before I see it—the cold water lapping around my feet. I can't tell where it's coming from, but there must be a hole in my canoe. It's not enough to sink me. But the water gets higher and higher as I paddle around the marker. I'm barely afloat when I finally cross the finish line. Kent has won for the Red Team. Woody wins second place for the Yellows. Buster, looking even smaller than usual in his oversized green T-shirt, is third. And I'm fourth, otherwise known as last. Everyone on my team is very disappointed.

Jamie, the sports counselor, sees my damaged canoe. He pulls it out of the lake and says he's sorry. "That's the way it goes." I ask about a do-over, but the next race is already starting and I end up sounding like a whiny loser.

For the rest of the day, I try to stay out of sight. I'm lying on my bunk, wondering whether to even go in for dinner when Jamie comes by. "Hunter, I need you to see something." He leads me over to the white boatshed by the lake where the canoes are kept. The "wet paint" sign is no longer on the door.

The counselor points to my wooden canoe. "Someone may have sabotaged you." He shows me the hole in the bottom, under the seat. It's perfectly round, not like something acci-dental or natural. "It was fine yesterday. But someone could have sneaked in after the schedule was posted. The flags were already on the canoes, and everyone knew you'd be the first kid to use it. Any ideas who did this?"

"I might be able to figure it out," I tell him. "I'm pretty good at this sort of thing."

Jamie says there's no real proof of sabotage, but if I come up with some evidence or a confession, then he'll arrange a do-over. I ask if I can look around the boatshed, and he says I can.

The shed has maybe thirty canoes, some on racks, some hanging from the freshly painted brown walls. There's a bench with repair supplies, including vices, hammers, and screwdrivers. There's also a little hand drill. I look down and see tiny shavings of dark wood in the seams between the floor planks. But this isn't proof. I also see a smudge on the wall, right by where my canoe is hanging. It looks like someone had leaned against the paint while it was still wet. This might be a clue.

Tonight in the dining room I sit with my team, picking at my lasagna and keeping an eye on my suspects. Everyone has changed out of their team T-shirts, but we still hang out together. Kent Tillis, the canoe race winner, seems to be reliving his victory, laughing and flailing his arms, like he's making fun of a drowning person. Me, undoubtedly.

Buster Hennessy is at his own team table, scarfing down his second helping of lasagna. It's amazing that a kid so skinny can eat so much and not put on an ounce of weight or an inch in height. Meanwhile, Woody, at the yellow table, has changed into a camouflage sweatshirt and no longer looks like a banana. He's chatting with a girl and picking at what looks like a bug bite on his neck.

I glance back and forth to all three of them. Then the solution comes to me. The cheater made a mistake. And with any luck, maybe he hasn't gotten rid of the evidence yet.

Can you solve this one?
Who drilled the hole in Hunter's canoe?
What evidence is Hunter looking for?

Solution on page 94

solution to "who emptied the candy jar?"
Page 5

There's no one around, but still, I lean in and whisper. "It was Ginny."

Logan makes a face. "I know Ginny loves to shop. What makes you think she's a thief?"

"Because of the cookies. Ginny said she brought cookies for everyone on the committee, right? But she didn't bring one for Brian. She obviously knew he wouldn't be there."

Logan smiles. "I guess I noticed, too, but it didn't seem important. Leave it to Hunter Monroe."

I'm worried that this is going to get Ginny into trouble, but Logan takes care of it. Before dinner, he goes over to Ginny's and comes back with the missing money. After dinner, he walks over to Brian's and returns the money. He tells them an anonymous friend of the band heard about the robbery and donated enough to make up for it.

Brian and his family believe Logan, of course. Everyone believes Logan.

solution to "The Key to the Test"
Page 9

"Was it Jocelyn or Peter?" Logan asks. We're halfway down the hall, all by ourselves.

"Neither," I tell him. "It was Mr. Johnson."

Logan is relieved. "And you know this from the warm key?"

I nod. "The key couldn't have been sitting in the locker. It would have been cold. The easiest way it could be warm was if someone was holding it. I think Mr. Johnson had the key in his hand. When he pretended to search Peter's locker, he dropped it."

"So, he's the one who stole the tests? A security guard?"

"Why not?" I say. "He had access to Mom's office. I guess he was planning to sell the answers. But when he made his mistake with the key and the copier, he knew he had to blame someone else."

Logan looks back to the lockers where Jocelyn and Pete are still arguing and a whole crowd is looking on. "Do you want to take credit for this one? You really should."

I seriously consider it for about three seconds. "No thanks. Maybe next time."

solution to "How Timmy Got Better"
Page 13

"You haven't been in bed all day," I tell Timmy. "While your mom was working, you got bored. You sneaked down the back stairs and took Goldie out. Probably through the kitchen door where your mom wouldn't see you."

"I did not," he says.

"Then how did Goldie's paws get dirty?"

"What do you mean?"

"When I came in, Goldie jumped up and got dirt on me. But your mom said the dog hadn't been out since this morning. If she'd been in the house, the dirt would have worn off. I'm thinking you took her out in the backyard, probably in the last half hour."

My best friend looks embarrassed and guilty. Also a little scared. "Don't tell Mom, please."

"Why are you doing it? I thought you liked school." Timmy's always been a great student, doing his homework early and raising his hand. I've even seen a couple of seventh grade boys teasing him about being a teacher's pet.

And then it hits me. "Are you being bullied?" I ask. He doesn't admit it, but I can tell. "We have to tell your parents and the school. My mom has handled bullying before. It's not your fault."

And for once, my best friend listens to me.

solution to "The Double Mugging"
Page 16

I'm nervous about telling a real cop my weird theory. But I clear my throat and start. "When we were at the first attack, you said something about the victim fighting back."

"That's right," says Uncle J.B. "There were defensive wounds and some blood."

"Well, what if the mugger got injured? I mean, really injured. He would need to go to a hospital. But he couldn't, because then he'd be a suspect."

Our uncle agrees. "We always check emergency rooms when there's a violent crime."

"So, he had to find a way to get to the hospital without becoming a suspect."

"Are you saying the second victim…Wow!" Logan knows I'm right.

"He wasn't a victim," I say. "He was the mugger. He hid the knife and his bloody sweatshirt and cap. He also had to hide the wallets, in order for his story to make sense. His main concern was to save his own life and not get arrested."

Uncle J.B. isn't as easily convinced. "That's a good theory. But you have no proof."

"I have a little proof," I say. "We all saw the first mugger. He had on a black top and a cap."

"Right," says Uncle J.B. "And that's how the second victim described him."

"No," I say. "He said the mugger was wearing a Yankees cap. But he couldn't have known it was a Yankees cap. Not unless he saw the mugger from the front, which he says he didn't."

Officer J.B. Monroe is impressed. "It may not be enough for a conviction, but it's certainly enough to get a subpoena for a DNA test. Maybe I should take you guys on more ride-alongs."

"Great," says Logan, erupting into a grin. "Just don't tell Mom."

solution to "The Vanishing Phone"
Page 20

Logan doesn't seem very excited by my news. "What does it matter?" he says. "If it was a prank or a theft or if the phone got lost, Derrick's getting a new one."

"It probably matters a lot," I say, "though I'm just guessing why Uncle Nigel did it."

"Uncle Nigel?" Now I have Logan's attention.

"It has to be," I say. "Everyone else saw Derrick put the

phone under the drone. But the thief looked under cushions and in drawers and in closets. Uncle Nigel's the only person who would need to search. Plus, I think he lied about his business call to Hong Kong. It's the middle of the night there. Like 4:00 a.m."

"I'm confused," says Logan. "Why would he steal Derrick's phone and then buy him a new one?"

"Because of something on the phone." I'm guessing here, but it's a good guess. "Remember how he didn't want the drone taking a video of him? Derrick was going to post it on Facebook. Maybe Uncle Nigel is into some shady deals and he doesn't want his face and name plastered all over social media."

It's an easy theory for us to check. We go back in the house. Logan secretly takes a photo of Uncle Nigel and we lift his prints from a water glass. Then we take it to our own uncle, J.B. Monroe of the Clifton Lake P.D.

By the next morning we have our answer. Turns out Uncle Nigel is a con artist, wanted in Texas and hiding out with his family for a while until things cool down.

Derrick's family is really upset, but Derrick takes it okay. After all, he has his new phone.

solution to "The case of the ghostly Note"
Page 25

They're all listening to me for a change. "First off, there are no ghosts. One of you made the sound, not the knife."

Sophie isn't buying it. "If one of us made the sound, then

how did the knife get into the door? That would have made a sound, too."

"Right," I say. "So it couldn't be you, Sophie. We would have heard you. Also, Timmy would have definitely seen it when he came back from the bathroom."

"Hey, it wasn't me," says Timmy.

"It wasn't you," I agree. "And for the same reason. We would have heard you stabbing the door."

"And it couldn't have been me," says Gloria. "For the same reason."

"Actually, it was you." Gloria throws me a deadly scowl, but I go on. "If it wasn't a ghost—and it wasn't—then the door was never stabbed."

"But you all saw it," Gloria insists. "The knife and the note."

"No. By the time we looked, the knife wasn't in the door. It was in your hand. You must have set it up before, making a knife hole in the door, then hiding the note and the knife somewhere. When you left the room, looking for the ghost, you had a few seconds to take them out and fool us."

Gloria doesn't admit to anything. But Timmy knows I'm right. "You gouged the door," he yells at his sister. "I'm telling Mom."

solution to "Logan's Big Moment"
Page 29

How could Logan have a piece of information that I don't? We both saw, heard, and touched the same things. And then it hits me. Logan must have smelled something that I didn't because of my cold. I remember now that the intruder had spilled a bottle of body spray—and that Logan wrinkled his own nose in Charlotte's room when he smelled it.

"It was Sebastian," I deduce. "He's the only brother we talked to in person. Noah never let us in and Charlie was in the library. You smelled Charlotte's body spray on Sebastian."

"I'd recognize her body spray anywhere," Logan says with a dreamy look on his face. "And it was all over Sebastian."

solution to "The Mystery of the Roses"
Page 33

"How did the roses get snipped?" I ask them. It sounds like a dumb question, but it's not. "A pair of regular scissors couldn't do it. And I don't think the culprit went into the shed, used the shears, and then cleaned them off and returned them. Not when he could get caught any second."

I can see the confusion on Ms. Finkelton's face. "You mean my nephew and niece planned this in advance? They brought their own pruning shears?"

"Why would they bring their own shears when yours are right here? No, Quincy brought them." And before anyone can react, I grab my new friend's backpack and unzip it. There, under his books and homework, is a pair of garden shears, still wet with the sticky sap.

Quincy looks shocked. Then he smirks. "I guess you are a detective, after all."

"Quincy? You did it? Why?" Ms. Finkelton asks. "And how?"

"He was playing a prank," I say. "Quincy threw the Frisbee into the tree on purpose. Then he made up the story about your roses. When I went around to the front, Quincy dropped over the fence, cut the roses and climbed back over. It took him just a couple of minutes. The result was a mystery he thought would stump me for good."

Quincy doesn't look very sorry. "I made a mistake with the shears."

"Not just the shears. The thorns." I point to his jacket. "I was wondering why you took the time to put on your jacket, especially on a warm afternoon."

Now, finally, Quincy looks impressed. He takes off his jacket and shows us his wounds, the little scratches and blood spots on his arms and wrists, where the thorny rose bushes left their marks.

solution to "Tree-slaughter in the First Degree"
Page 38

Both my uncle and my best friend are waiting. "It was the last suspect," I tell them. "Mr. Eversol was lying."

"What was the clue?" asks Timmy.

"There are actually two clues," I say. "First, he claimed that he saw Mr. Taylor at home all morning. But I found some sawdust in Mr. Taylor's car tires, meaning he must have driven home after the tree was cut down."

My uncle smiles. "So, Mr. Taylor was telling the truth about his alibi."

"Right. But the big clue is what Mr. Eversol could see

from his treadmill. Or couldn't see. Before the tree was cut down, Mr. Eversol had almost no view from his bedroom window. It would have been impossible for him to see Mr. Taylor in his garage, or Ms. Elway and her dogs."

Officer J.B. Monroe is impressed—and a little puzzled. "I thought Logan was the detective in the family."

solution to "a case of the sparkles"
Page 43

Band class is starting, so I tell Logan and Jocelyn to meet me after school at the lockers. For the rest of the day, I enjoy having this secret. And when I leave my last class and turn the corner to the row of lockers, they're waiting for me.

"Open your locker," I tell Jocelyn, without even saying please. I'm thinking there must be an umbrella in there and I'm right. "I guess it could have been Fiona or Hugo," I say. "But the fact that this only happens when it's raining, gives us a much better suspect." And with that, I take out Jocelyn's little red umbrella and open it.

"Don't. It's bad luck," Jocelyn says. But she stops protesting when she sees two specks of glitter fall out of the umbrella. Logan starts laughing. Then I laugh. Even Jocelyn breaks into a grin. "My evil little brother."

"You have to admit, it's clever," I say. "All Tony has to do is put glitter inside your umbrella. Then when you're leaving the house and it's raining and you're all worried about getting wet, you don't even notice it falling on your head."

solution to "the old teapot"

Page 47

"Who was that man?" I ask. "The one who wanted the teapot." It's a few minutes later and Uncle J.B. is standing with us in Al's Emporium. He's been listening to everyone's story and taking notes.

"That was Norm DeMarco," says Ms. Culpepper. "He owns a real antique shop, over by the freeway."

"Norm walked by the shop yesterday and saw the teapot." Mr. Simmons lets out an evil little laugh. "He came in and offered me ten bucks, like he was doing me a favor. Like he didn't already know. I kicked him out, just like that."

I nod to Logan and let him take over. Logan's better at explaining things, and people tend to believe him.

"Mr. DeMarco is your thief," says Logan. "He knew how rare the teapot was and that you didn't have much security. This morning, after the snow stopped, he climbed up to the roof, dropped in, stole the teapot and the money from the cash register."

Al Simmons is skeptical. "If he'd already taken the teapot, like you say, then why did he come back and ask about it?"

"Because he'd forgotten his gloves. Remember? Mr. DeMarco was rubbing his hands together when he walked in. Yet he picked up a pair of gloves before walking out. He had to come back because he thought the gloves might be a clue."

"That's true," Officer J.B. says. "Sometimes you can get prints from inside a glove, even a leather glove. Good work, Logan."

Logan blushes. And that makes me smile.

solution to "Two Perfect Alibis"
Page 52

"Who is it?" Logan asks. "Is it Sonny? Or is someone lying about their alibi?"

"Neither. Both alibis are valid, and Sonny's telling the truth." It's all I can do to keep from laughing. "Just think about what Sonny said. He said he was on the bench press machine. Then he heard the noise and looked up at the clock."

"So?"

"So the weight machine faces the mirror. If Sonny saw the clock, it had to be reflected in the mirror. I'll bet you anything the time wasn't 11:55 but 12:05, ten minutes later. This also explains why he wound up being late to his next class."

This time we both laugh out loud. "I'll bet you're right," says Logan.

Logan and I rethink the alibis. Brenda was in the cafeteria at 12:05, according to her friends and according to Coach Iverson. But Jeremy's alibi only lasts until noon, when he left class. He had five full minutes to meet his friends and sneak into the equipment room for a quick smoke.

"Sonny's going to be pretty embarrassed when we tell him."

"Don't worry," says Logan. "I'll take care of it."

solution to "Band Room Revenge"
Page 56

We're sitting in the principal's office, telling Mom our theory. "Mr. Ashton painted those horrible things about himself?" She shakes her head. "No, it doesn't make sense."

"I know," I say. "But it had to be done by someone with the alarm code. And only you and Mr. Ashton know the code, right?"

"That's right, but…"

I keep talking. "Mr. Turnabene says that from the time he heard the alarm to the time you both got there, it was only two minutes. That gave the culprit just two and a half minutes to do all the damage. That's pretty impossible."

Mom gives this some thought. "Well, maybe there were several culprits. If they were fast and had figured everything out ahead of time…"

"But all the graffiti is in the same handwriting," I say. "I think Mr. Ashton yelled at us on purpose, and then painted that stuff. Then he triggered the alarm just as he was leaving."

"Why would he do that?"

I honestly don't know, but I have a theory. "So he could cancel the trip to Burlingate High."

Logan helps me out. "You know how Mr. Ashton is always bragging about how he was such a great director and wrote this great march? Well, what if he's lying? The last thing he would want is for all of us to go to his old school and find out the truth."

"I'll check this out," says Mom. She's impressed by our logic. "You're both very clever boys. I'm proud of you."

It may be my imagination, but I think she's looking straight at me.

solution to "The unlocked Bike"
Page 60

We're back in the house. Mrs. Whitford yelled at us for a full minute, then gave us towels and sent us to the laundry room. Logan and I are okay, but Casey has to put his clothes in the dryer and borrow something from Derrick.

As soon as we're alone, Casey turns to me. "Okay, who stole my bike?"

Before I can say anything, Logan speaks up. "Hunter, wait. I know you're a pretty great detective, but there's something you don't know." He looks nervous.

"Well, I know that you're the one who took Casey's bike."

Casey's mouth drops open. Logan is also a little shocked. "How did you know?"

"Because your rain slicker was on top of one of the coat hooks."

Logan thinks it over and nods. "That's a fair clue."

Casey doesn't know what we're talking about, so I explain. "Logan was one of the early people at the party. His slicker would be near the bottom of the pile. But when Logan and I went outside to investigate, Logan grabbed his slicker from the top. That means he'd been outside again when no one was looking. And the only reason I can think for him to go out in this rain would be to move your bike to a safer place."

"Sorry, Casey." Logan is pretty embarrassed. "I moved your bike around to the side and locked it. I was hoping to teach you a lesson about safety. I guess I didn't count on my smarty-nose brother figuring it out."

solution to "science fair sabotage"

Page 64

Nicholas still wants to call the police, but I take him aside and whisper in his ear. As soon as the Olsen family drives off down the street, he turns and asks, "Why do you think it was me?" His voice is shaking.

"Well, you said it happened last night—when you assumed we'd all be asleep and not have good alibis."

"That's when it did happen," says Nicholas. "I heard the break-in."

"No," I tell him. It happened just an hour ago. When Timmy and I took out your garbage, the bin was pretty full. You said that the garbage truck comes around 7:00 a.m. And sure enough, when you and I looked inside, there was no garbage—except your science project, which you threw out this morning."

"That's stupid," he says. "Why would I destroy my own invention?"

"Because it doesn't work, not the way you've been saying. The judges would see that. This morning you finally gave up. You figured your only way out would be to invent a break-in and give yourself an excuse. You didn't care that one of your friends might get accused."

Despite this, I feel sorry for Nicholas and promise not to tell anyone. In a way, it's kind of good news, I think. But even without Nicholas, I don't win the science fair. Gloria wins with her study of the respiration of goldfish.

solution to "The case of the stolen diamond"
Page 68

I tell Uncle J.B. that I solved the case, but he's not buying it. "No, Hunter. It could have been anyone walking by and noticing the ring on the seat."

"That's not how it happened," I say, "because I would have heard the glass breaking. And I didn't hear a thing."

J.B. Monroe knows I'm a very observant kid, and when I swear that the night was perfectly silent before the car alarm started, he believes me. "What are you saying, that the window was broken before Chet Galinski drove up?"

"No," I say. "The rock is from his garden. The glass on the street is from his car window. Plus, he has no motive to steal his own ring and damage his BMW."

"Then why didn't anyone hear the window break?"

"Because it was broken after the alarm started. The alarm covered up the noise."

My uncle considers this seriously. "You're saying the alarm was a false alarm, after all?"

"It happens, right?"

"And when Randy Smith came out to check the false alarm, he noticed the ring box on the seat. He smashed the window. And no one heard because the alarm was already blaring."

I nod yes. "He wouldn't have had time hide it. So if you can get Mr. Smith to consent to a search, you'll probably find the ring in his jacket pocket."

solution to "Hunter and the Blue canoe"
Page 73

Even though we're having strawberry shortcake tonight, and it's my absolute favorite, I leave the dining room before dessert and track down Buster Hennessy's cabin on the far side of the field.

The camp is on the honor system here, so all the cabins are unlocked. I feel guilty for breaking in, but I know I'm right about Buster. He's the one who sneaked into the boatshed while the paint was still wet. He's the one who accidentally leaned against the wall while he drilled the hole in my canoe. And he's the one who must have got paint on his team shirt, the same color paint used in the boatshed.

Buster's T-shirt was the last green, size small in the camp. He couldn't very well show up for the race with brown paint on his shirt. So he went into the meeting hall and took a large one from the shelf, the only size that was left. I noticed him wearing the new shirt this morning, right before the race, but I didn't connect it until later.

After everyone else has had their strawberry shortcake and left the dining hall, I go to the counselors' main cabin and explain my theory to Jamie. Then I pull out the T-shirt I found in the bottom of Buster's duffel bag—a Green Team shirt, size small, with a brown smear of paint all along the back. Jamie is upset that I broke into Buster's duffel. But he's even more upset with Buster.

The next morning, we redo the canoe race, with someone

else from the Green Team taking Buster's place. I still come in fourth. But at least it's an honest fourth.